The Blue Field

BARBARA KLAR

COTEAU BOOKS

Edited by Gerry Hill.

Cover design by The Noblet Design Group.
Book design by Karen Thomas.
Author photo by Hal Gates.
Printed and bound in Canada.

The publisher gratefully acknowledges the financial assistance of the
Saskatchewan Arts Board, the Canada Council for the Arts, the
Department of Canadian Heritage, and the City of Regina Arts
Commission, for its publishing program.

Canadian Cataloguing in Publication Data

Klar, Barbara, 1966–
The blue field
ISBN 1-55050-148-8

I. Title.
PS8571.L367B48 1999   C811'.54   C99-920027-5
P9199.3.K466B48 1999

COTEAU BOOKS
401-2206 Dewdney Ave.
Regina, Saskatchewan
Canada   S4R 1H3

AVAILABLE IN THE US FROM

General Distribution Services
85 River Rock Drive, Suite 202
Buffalo, New York,
USA 14207

for Hal

ONE

Two

ONE

THE BLUE FIELD

❀

Snow falls on the ghost
of June, the field deep
as flax after rain.

The sun falls no lower
than unashamed sadness,
shadow on blue snow.

Flowers have been lost.
The coldest months
are decades to the thaw.

✻

A trillion six-sided stars
fall and give off dusk.
Wine warm, I remove
my clothes, fold them
on the snow and lie down.

Tomorrow follow my tracks
and find my hands
folded over my pubis.
Cold is the tooth
of a wolf and then
cold is peace.

ONE TON

Country, you have shown me the crying
widow at the auction, her husband's red
'49 Fargo once, twice, sold.

Cold, you will have me love
the space between old women, heavy
as the news of death in winter.

Sky, you have asked me to buy you,
to adore absence. Unlike mountains
it demands only patience.

Country, you will teach me to not stare
when the widow's daughters walk her away.

DEER MOUSE

1.

I find the skull
whole, a dried white flower,
a stitch in a doiley, a she
in my hand, this day
of silence for things her size.

2.

Smallness has the eyes
of the deer she once was,
her body many times more acute.

Winter does not starve
the large-eyed mouse who sights
food in the dark.

3.

Lighter than an ounce, the deer mouse
skims her acre for dry weeds
taller than snow. The seed coats
of last fall's sowthistle spin
from her claws. The new moon feast
is hers until the owl
dives and the heart
of the deer mouse waits under snow.

4.

Snow takes
the drag marks of tails:
stems.
The prints of feet:
ovate leaves.
Mice have told me vines are good.

5.

The morning after snow I sink
across the field. Boots
are the feet of an elephant.
To leave shallow tracks
I would weigh less
than an ounce, keep
walking south.

Owls sleep in tree bones.
The deer mice beat
below their summer tracks.

THE CLASSIFICATION OF SNOW
for Marshall

Precipitated snow reveals
the purity of flight. No two
loop-the-loops are the same.
Every stellar crystal lands
as it may. Six wings graze
a cabin window. Six wings
softly light on your roof.

Metamorphosed snow loses
perfection now that it lives
on earth. Think of it as metal
rusting in a heavy pile, shape
no longer discernable, a way
to mention death.

Non-precipitated crystals sublimate
on earth. The saving grace of cold
is not really snow at all
but ash that never fell.

The Woodcutter

Lesson 1

Winter is a boulder.
She would accept its weight
but stays inside, tries
to push it from her path.

Lesson 2

Through mica windows
the fire is her television,
her stare still as a cold front.

Through the other window
his eight-pound splitting maul
blurs through the air, stopped
only by the chopping block.

Split, laughs every log, falling
from its centre. And between each split
the silent arc of muscle, rhythm, talent.

Lesson 3

His maul, heavy as winter,
is just an extension
of his right arm.

Lesson 4

How much wood could a woman split
if a woman could split wood?
Enough to keep the house
warmer than this, to desire
him and not another blanket.

She desires to be
the woodcutter, strong
like her husband.

Lesson 5

It's about speed, he says.
Start the swing above
your head, get the maul going
a hundred miles an hour, swing it through
the log like the log ain't there.

She barely lifts the maul.
Her slow swing misses. The log
falls, whole. She falls, broken.

Lesson 6

Her logs remain whole but her arms
thicken. *It's about the maul,* she says.
She swings its eight pounds at nothing
a thousand times a day behind
the big tree where he
cannot watch her.

Lesson 7

She desires to aim
not for the log but the chopping block,
to swing through the coldest air. Even she
might split brittle wood.
Today she aims. Today
she swings fast. The steel head
halves the log which crashes to earth
in two opposing pieces.

She is warm except for the fingers
on her right hand, the sky
so clear it burns.

Lesson 8

She splits wood as if her husband
is not there. As if she is
the only woodcutter

and spring is just a rock
she moves forward so she can stand
under winter and be
not cold.

LIBERTY FIRE EXTINGUISHER
a poem found in the unburned house

Pull down quickly
thus removing cap
Holding tube firmly
hurl contents
forcibly with
clubbing motion into
base of flames
repeating strokes
rapidly
For flue fires
throw contents into
any opening below
the flames

Always strike
forcibly
never sprinkle

Price $4.00

Weight 3 Pounds

Hang On Strong Hook

Maytag Gyrator II, Patented 1952

1.

I begin to curse its slowness but not the wives before me,
the stout ones with thick arms from lifting babies and wet
laundry. In the early mornings their voices still grind at
their husbands and sons. Those red ghosts are hands
pinning diapers to the line behind the lilacs.

2.

She kneels on the concrete floor,
scrubs my father's overalls
with a nail brush, drops them
in the wringer washer
she has no need to replace.

3.

This one comes with our house, leaking oil on the
basement floor who knows how long. You gaily get it
running, feed our rinsed socks through the rollers, a few
at a time. *Good as driving my old truck*, you say, my lover
of archives.

Start, stop.
Forward, reverse.
Push to release.
Every Monday morning I drive with our clothes through
the country of warm grey water.

4.

I know the story of a boy
whose mother feeds his hand
through the wringer just for lying.
Hers is the story of wringing away
the truth. *I turned my back*
for one second, he wanted
to see how the damn thing worked.

5.

I have not searched the basement
for bones. Mine is the story
of the 1950s housewife whose washer
wrings out light.

THAW

The church between towns is seldom used, frozen since December. By March it has become one of those high drifts in the middle of flatness, its steeple smoothed over by the snow blowing across the grid, piling up toward heaven. Inside, the fir floor glints with frost, a stoic glacier only just moving in the direction of spring.

The mice and spiders have left. Even Jesus has left for somewhere warmer. In the church between towns, the sleeping black flies are the only things living though their frozen bodies seem dead.

Henry White dies and the furnace is lit, three days to the funeral. The ceiling joists make cracking sounds as they warm and expand. The cream-coloured walls appear through the frost, starting at the top, spreading toward the baseboards. The pews and the floor lose their whiteness. The wood glows a bit like sunshine.

The flies swivel their heads, twitch their legs, lift their wings.

The church smells like cake and flowers. Mourners drive through a March storm to sing their tears to Henry and the thawed-out organ's music. By now the flies are buzzing against the stained glass and doing figure eights around the ceiling fans. Outside, the last of winter rages, but inside, Henry's old brother is reading at the altar. *Henry was a kind man who loved nature and gardening. Henry never hurt a fly.* His coffin is wheeled out into the storm and the flies watch from above the voices.

Henry White has died and the day after the funeral the furnace is shut off. Above the church, Henry's soul hears the music of the flies buzzing over the cake crumbs, the flies eating and sleeping on the warmth of the south windowsills now that the sun is out. New snow is melting into Henry's grave.

April Sixteenth

Say it has been decades
since you thawed. Your eyes
are ice with no meaning
for heat. Even music cannot bend
your limbs without breaking them.

Watch the field cry off
its snow. There is hope
for both of you. Watch winter fall
as a house might burn, an event
even to the frozen. Say
it has been decades since you ran
toward puddles as if they were flames.

THAW

Water's joy
flows forward under ice.
Sun and water rub
ice into water
and the mountain
sends down more.

This river could have been
about sex without my ever
saying. The first bone
shows on the inside
of my south-facing thigh.

NINE REASONS

The sky on clear days
is a pleasing colour. The sun
pleases ice. Rivers thaw,
liquid as my blood. I am
cold liquid. I could drown in myself.

The sun rises. Temples
rise, for centuries. They sound
like architects thinking.
I should jump from the top
of a question, break my bones.

I'm not fat.
I like dogs.
I walk to the river.
My blood is a pleasing colour.

DECREATION STORY

Dark and its stars and no moon
shine. Night is still a tall black woman
with lamps in her skin, her sad, confident
skin.

Night still waits for her half-sister.
They take turns staying with their mother,
the old one, the earth and fire
barely breathing.

Night sings to their mother,
brings her wine, rubs her with the oils
of flowers. Night and her lamps
and no moon shine, her half-sister climbs
the hills to meet her, to hold her
as the children of the old ones
do.

Goodnight, Night. And Night
lies down. Her lamps go out in her skin,
earth and fire barely breathe.

THE BLUE FIELD

❀

Flax blooms with the grace
of water. Yes, water blooms. Ice
breaks into pale blue petals. Again
the lakes flower.

From a distance you call
the field blue water
next to sky.

❀

Yes, flax ripples. Your eye
will want to cross it by canoe,
the journey of the year
that requires only wind.

✤

The field will let you dream
of harvest if you let it
dream of linen.

The east weaves light,
turns it west, closes
flowers on the stalks
you will hold in many years.

✤

Dawn is blue but this
is the earliest blue. Like all
forms of summer, flax parts
while you sleep. Five
small, overlapping petals know
more than you when they open.

You have chosen to be
a peasant. Flax is your wife.
What it does
it does before the sun
climbs any higher.

BODY OF MANY BLUE WINGS

after a line by Gwendolyn MacEwen

Many blues come before this
pale blue field, this body
of turning wings. They kiss
the air with the sound
that has been done, blue's
calm vowel, its handy ambiguity
for anything: blue fire, blue morning,
blue eyes, sadness, suicide, moons, windows.

I want to explain why
blue is overused, but too much blue
kills the bluebird a shade
too close to sky.

Raspberries

Again you keep the sun from going down.

Thawed raspberries bleed a happy blood
through cheesecloth. Remember the blood
of half a year ago? The canes
dripped raspberries. Your bare feet
crushed the fallen ones. The rest
bled into your pails.

This

    will be wine
for your winter mouth.
Sugar and juice push
their steam from an iron pot
to the window. You cannot see
out but it is day.

Red

    is the sweetest month.
You dig thorns from the horizon,
wash the seeds off your feet.
The water turns July.

THE BIRD

Raspberries, she sang, are the nipples
of women who have loved too much,
bleeding from the tongues of many men.

Did the men love well? I asked.

Well, she sang. But they did not
stay long. The women cried and grew
thorns, hid in the orchard where no men
could reach them or leave them.

She sang, and my hands
stopped moving. More
over-ripe berries dropped.

Are the nipples tears, falling?

Falling scabs, she sang.

Birthday Bear

1.

I rise in the forest
on my birthday. Yards in front
of my tent, last year's cub
licks at a plate, stands
on its hind legs, sniffs the air
for what I am.

Twenty-nine, I would dance with it.

2.

I begin to believe
in the births of bears.

Frost echoes around
the birthing room, a pit

where a poplar has lifted its roots.
The sow knows what is happening,

grunts when the second cub
plops out and steams.

3.

In the hospital run by nuns
I was a summer baby given a bear
with a bow around its neck.

4.

I begin to believe
in a four-month sleep, a yearling
curled against mother and twin,
hearts torpid, the den damp
with their barely breathing.

For their birthdays in winter
I will think of bears turning
two and five and ten in their sleeps.

FLYING

for the heli-crew

August 18, 8 a.m.

My first time. Sky pounds my back. I crouch in the sand 190 miles north-east of Slave Lake, Alberta, chopper blades chopping sky as if sky were a solid, an apple or a carrot, sky falling in red and orange pieces. Only when the chopper lands and cuts its rotors does its windshield shine, the compound eyes of a dragonfly. I stand.

August 18, 9 a.m.

All aboard. The pilot. *The way through swamps is above them.* We rise and tilt west, lean into the vector of our next contract. Two foremen, two cooks, the first load of planters with their shovels across their hearts. And this is not apocalypse.

August 18, 10 a.m.

The ground is a puzzle with half its pieces missing. This must be how fields begin, the stubble of cut trees. I am in the sky, then below it. I have been in the mountains and on the prairie.

August 18, 9 p.m.

Camp up. Our only neighbours are those dead pines by the swamp, the brooms of witches pointing at the moon on our first night.

August 20, 4 a.m.

Fog seeps into my waking. The rest of camp is asleep. I have stretched a rope from my tent to the cook tent, a guide through the dark to my work. Even in a clear-cut reached only by air there is breakfast.

August 22, 2 p.m.

It has taken me till now to realize what brought us here. Not a dragonfly but a stork, dropping sling after sling of equipment and baby trees, *C-GRHW* printed in huge black against its orange belly. And when it left us here, a heart thumped away, distant then absent. The start of isolation not yet acknowledged. Mosquito silence. A Bell 204 ½ no longer ringing.

August 24, 8 p.m.

Ugly as it is, this wasteland is home. Today it thunder-showered and the planters walked in early, wet, cold, and content. Loneliness is like rain, that German poet said. The steady, falling self.

August 25, 9 p.m.

Strange how one strives for civilization here. Peanut butter hors d'oeuvres and fruit salads. I delivered raisin cookies to the block because I am the mother lonely in a kitchen.

August 26, 10 p.m.

The stork slung in more trees today, enough to finish the contract. I washed my hair, first time since we got here, put a skirt on. Cleanliness made me think of flying out, how to land back in the world.

August 28, 8 p.m.

Nearly dark this early, even in northern Alberta. The under-brush is turning red. Tons of wild blueberries in a nearby burn. I share my sleeping bag again tonight with no one but a spider whose back is pale yellow. The dusk of three colours is late summer here.

August something, 4 p.m.

In the shade of the cook tent. Dates are gone with what I remember of roads. This far along, anything man-made seems like a joke, that freezer in the fireweed, the cutlines that try to chop up the North into something we can han-dle. In the desert of this missing piece, there are no right angles.

August 30, 11 p.m.

We fly out tomorrow. Too tired to stay at the party. I baked the crew a cake in the shape of a helicopter.

August 31, 8 a.m.

Window seat. We push the sky down on half a million newly planted seedlings. An hour from now we'll know what streets are.

AUGUST THIRTY-FIRST

Earth is oven. Fields
smell of ready bread.
Apples darken on trees hot
to the touch.

          Open the door,
take them in. On this
early evening the strangers
in your house would eat.

THE POTATO WITH TWO HEADS

The beauty of the potato with arms
is no question. This garden
prefers to grow chaos.
Three carrots braid into one,
cucumbers meld at their hips, a potato
pushes a leg through the rust
of a safety pin dropped
in the dirt years ago.

This garden knows
the misshapen are happy. They stifle
their giggles underground, protect
the joke of old seed.

I am the potato with two heads
digging up my sisters.

Yellow On Blue

Leaves burn. Cold
begs fire. *I am cold*,
says September. *Warm me.*
And the leaves

light, reach toward
a child, in need
of her wish
for a burning.

Leaves burn. Blue begs
fire. The sky is coldest
at the start of cold,
the clearest blue. *Please.*

Leaves burn, old.
You are the last fires.
Slow the coldness, the sky
bright and later, mother.

THREE WEEKS

There is a hole in the year
where, a year ago, we gathered.
I will call the place *goldenness*.
We were the leaves
of nine related species on one tree
taking light from the fields
that would not stop shining.
But the precious fell.
The wind blew east and west,
us to our cloudy basements.

In the dream of not parting
we won't all fit in my truck
and no one gets to the airport.
That is not how it happened.
There was harvest. Fields
went out. I will call
these weeks a hole in the year
where we shone before parting.

GIFT DAYS

The field spends weeks
thanking itself, a pleased
exhaustion slowly freezing
like the river but still
moving forward.

I could get more sentimental
than that. *The sun rolls
down the sky's blue cheek.*
The field receives neither
autumn nor winter, limbo
nor motion but the absence
of falling snow.

Like the days we ask
for little but our summer selves
falling for once slowly.

November First

Ghosts have crossed the first snow.
October was disguised, a too long
summer. *Goodbye*, dreams the house
full of candy and potatoes.

Ghosts sleep, white
and certain, children
in a house itself again.
The truth falls on the fields
and loves us all.

December Twenty-First

The dusks have made me
fall with the sun and rise
before it, the dark not remembering
but anticipating light.
Early to rise: to mend
a glove below a lamp,
hear the hand open.

Fielding

To face the wind
of questions. To catch the ball
and know where to throw it.
To lean like the road sign
beside the leaning town east
of here. To cross white space
on snowshoes. To cross clover
to the shoulders, leave no path.

Two

RETURNING

Away for six years, I reek
of the lonely, cry
until my eyes bleed.
I crawl back to what I must
believe is love, your bare room
where grace is up to me.

You smell the others
on my hands. They kept me
gone and bleeding.
Absence seemed painless.

Am I welcome?
Your room fills with my smell.
Nothing sends me away.

The Cloak

Stones are tied to my body.
They cover my bruises but make me
weigh. My skin stretches groundward.
Bruises made the stones, not vice versa.
From their fear they threw
anchors out to safety. Slowly,
I move, stones swinging from
my neck. They hit me
and my skin retracts.

The Bent Woman

❀

My spine is a bone
road through the mountains.
I despise unstraightness.
Drive down my humps. My hate
crumbles the granite beneath you.

❀

The caterpillar coils under
a stick. The bird tucks
into her wing, a twist
so tight nothing enters.

❀

I turn away from mirrors, know
how bent I am by my feet
at different angles, the torque
of my pelvis. Once when I smiled
a rib scraped my heart.

❀

The tall ones were here
first. I gnarl toward
the sun and wait for it
to straighten me.
Jack pine is crippled
but jack pine is stone.

FOUR WORDS FOR MY BODY

Hole

I fall through the hole
of my mouth, do not cry out
from the bottom of me.
My life is filling the hole
deeper with every bite,
filling the shaft of my heart.

Cow

To the cow who eats herself
to death, her only love is pasture.
Another acre of food consoles me,
confirms my ugliness, loves despite
my ugliness.

Skinny

What enters must not stay.
One fall I come back from tree planting weighing
less than in grade six, full
of work instead of food.

Belly

You look like you're fucking pregnant.
Your words when you find me sprawled
on our bed like a naked drunk,
when my blood sugar
spins the room above my belly
long after my disgust
in me was born.

CANDIDIASIS

❀

My cunt is sore.

❀

Bats breed in the cave
of me. What oozes out
screeches. Yeast cells
are the black of me,
not mammal, not bird.

❀

I am infested, a woman
on a mountain in a poor country,
spreading my legs to the salves
of a holy man. I am swollen
shut. You love me outside me,
lay your hand there as if
I am clean and those poems
were not lies.

❀

My cunt is a word
itching. If I scratch
long enough it will erase.

WHY I HATE CHILDREN

Because.

And because they had
nicer clothes, they played
when I sat still,
they whispered behind my back
about my hairy arms, fat cheeks,
split ends, pimples.
Because they loved to say
my name wrong and watch me turn
red. Because they held me
on the floor beside my grade three desk
and dumped glue in my hair.
Because I walked through the school
years later and the room
where they shoved my pencil up my nose
was still there, with their voices.

Because they were sad too.
Because I was sad I believed them.
Barbara is ugly.
Barbara is stupid.
Barbara can't ride a bike.
Because they laughed
the time I hated them.

THE CLIFF

We jumped. Or
loneliness pushed us. This
was love or death.

The rock split you open.
A desert puma, I
claw your wound,

hiss with a dry mouth.
This was one of two
mistakes. We lived. Loved.

Rock is our home,
your blood the only water.
Love made us fall.

The Pact

We agree on wine, on small
old buildings heated with fire,
these happy secrets of the sad.

Sameness, darkness,
and our first meeting: through
the holes in our clothes our skin

becomes stars. We agree to meet again
at night. And though we do not
say, to undress

each other in a place lit
by sameness, a star also.

THE NIGHT OF TOLD SECRETS

The night has come to this
wish to show you in, tell
a fine thing to your body.

Fear of laughter
locks my house.

The night ends not
inside but with the wish
that my last secret open.

WATCHING YOU CRY

Your eyes are deer
drowning in rain,

in two rivers breaking
your voice like a river breaks

land in two. *I am leaving,*
I say. This night of storm.

Cry like the sky cries, bravely,
like a man cries, beautifully

and seldom. *I'll miss you,* say
the rivers. *You bitch,* say the rivers.

Cry until your eyes close
and deer bend to drink there.

October Seventh

Only I would lie naked
in wheat. My heavy skin
loves the poke of harvest,
the swath whose stalks
compress below the body.

I lie down and you
walk on, unaware I do not
follow. The sun rolls
across me, burns off your smell.
I rise at dusk, leave
the indentation of a beast.

THE DRESS

Small breasts hang
inside a small dress.
The dress is not too small.
I mean small in the way
that makes you see much
of my skin and think of more.

The breasts are not too small.
They are small in the way
that being thirteen seems
not that long ago, that you
think me young and think of more.

Watch me dance. I am
shape under clothing.
My breasts are the curves
your palms would make
when the dress barely lands.

Oestrus

You have peeled the skin
from my skin and found the place
I bleed from. Between our bodies
and the snow lies my doeskin,
black and red plaid cotton,
once the leather of the female
fallow deer.

      I bleed around you
and onto not a *mackinaw* or *lumber jacket*
but *doeskin*, your synonym for female,
the skin around my skin to keep
out the non-forest.

      You break
branches. I stand still
long enough for you to hold
my running. Now that my skin
is off you enter
my blood like a root.

TWO WAYS

We have fallen through the year
to where sky scatters
flowers and a rope of suns
burns on the tree west of us. Or
it snows and we hang up
white and gold. Two ways
of seeing everything. Darkness
as darkness or darkness as light. Snow
as snow or flowers, morning brighter
than coal. At the bottom
of the year we hold
each other's ropes and fall
no further, bottom as beginning,
falling, or light.

Seven Storms

❀

The storm heaps
snow on the garden's bones.
Last year's sunflowers
are crosses blowing down.

❀

The storm swallows the lonely.
I slide down its white throat,
hear your echo on the telephone.

You're a quarter mile away and there
for the night, the road consumed.

❀

I am snow-blind, neighbourless
for two nights and a day.
The nearest house is lost
at storm, the woodpile
all I can see.

❀

The storm explains our hearts
lately. We exploded, drifted
toward truth. Big, red flakes
finally settled like chicken feathers.

Believe it, this
is love. We do not know until
we float whitely to the ground.

❀

You haven't hit the ditch in twenty years.
Tonight your truck skates
five spirals and leaves the ice.
The snowplough driver brings you home.

Thank you for your humility.
Thank me for my body, the island
in this ocean snow. Waves
roll across the fields,
crash at our doors
but our safety lasts all night.

❀

The storm smooths corners.
Curves forget the names of what
they bury. Our upside-down boat
becomes a drumlin, the dugout a bowl.

The world curves, all one
colour, one absence
of colour. White sun
snows down.

❀

Their safety lasts all night.
Those who'd never heard of this town
drink to it now in a hotel whose lights
just reach the highway.

After Planting

Darling, our work is done and now
we may lie down. I am seed in the earth

of your arms. Now you may
come into me from below,

the goodnesses of soil, sun
or rain from above. You pull

my thin leaves toward you,
hold them still, a moon

behind me on this shortest night.
Even in sleep I bend toward you.

THE CUTTING

The Death

On the garden of the scalp
hair dies away from its seeds.

I have always moved slowly.
Long, beautiful death

hangs down my back, pulls me,
brown, to the earth.

The Record

My past flows from the present
to my waist. I remember
to the ends of my hair,
paper dry from the sun.

The Ego

I am the lover
with hair to her thighs. Allow me
to drown you in rose-scented streams.

The Girl

Hair makes me
young, blows in the wind.
Hair keeps me girl, covers
my body so you will not see
the woman here. Hair
keeps me holding a rope
of braid like an arm.

The Poem

In the poem called
The Cutting, the braid
must be loved to be severed.

The Mother

The cutting will remember my mother's, her braid rolled in
tissue paper, laid in a shoe box and brought across the sea
in the trunk full of her life. Every few years she brings the
box down from the top shelf of the linen closet, opens it
like a jewellery box, shows me.

The Gift

The scissors shake in my hand.
I should have done this
last night when I was drunk.

Today I feel pain
again, give the braid to my other
hand, no blood in my hand.

The Body

The cutting does not grow
but leaves a stalk that wishes
for light all along. My back
appears out of shadow.

The Lightness

On the day called
loss, absence blows in the wind.

I hold the fine weight of nothing.

Your Mothers Wish You Well On Earth

Twenty-one women stare into
your sleep, seven versions
of your mother's mother, seven
of your mother, seven of you.
On the brick schoolhouse steps
twenty-one women pose
in not enough light, dusk

the grey of your Oma's seven
skirts. None of them smile.
Your mothers look down. Only
you are the happy ones. Twenty-one
women stand on the steps
of your sleep, the front row
you, giggling in diapers,

in a frilly dress,
your first bra,
your graduation gown,
in the arms of a man, giggling
in not enough light, with a suitcase
full of paper. You wish your mothers
well in heaven and you turn.

BED SONG

The dog guards its wild dance
of bedding down, a dance to the words
sister to wolves, the three
turned circles, now four,
now sure the shadow radius
holds no evil.

Sister to wolves has the only fangs
in the room. Sister to wolves
gives its bones to the floor
and caution to what will be yesterday.

THE SLEEPING DOG
for Uisge Beatha

❀

There is no awareness of ocean.
The dog's right front paw
washes over the left.
The third eyelid rolls in
and does not break.

❀

The hearth dog's legs
stretch to the Southern Hemisphere.
Nose to tail is the constant
from which the world is measured.

❀

The dog slopes, a great
brindle mountain of back.

Blood runs toward
the twitching stone.

❀

In the dream chase the bark
becomes whimper, the gallop
a tremble of legs. The dog wakes
above the rabbit's throat,
flexes hot toes.

❀

The sleeping dog lies, swears
its simple world of love
is truth. You would not begin
to tell it what you think of.

❀

Cold rises in the room
without a fire. Let there be
a sleeping dog whose breathing
reflects in your eyes.

LOVE POEM AND TRAIN
   for Hal Gates

> *If love was a train*
> *I think I would ride me a slow one.*
> *- Michelle Shocked*

1.

The train is prairie wailing,
spilling tons of black tears
across its face. Hear them.

2.

The wailing train was me.
June 12, 1970, 1 a.m.
I was asleep, you seventeen,
we hadn't met yet, wouldn't
for another twenty years.

I was not dreaming of you
and two friends flying past
Swanson, Saskatchewan, in a red half ton,
not of the train flying
at a right angle to the highway.
I was asleep,
barely dreaming of pain.

3.

The moving train at night
draws its black line
east across the dark.
I didn't see no train. Next thing I know,
up, down, sideways, nothing but train

and the hood
folds, a slow accordion,
the steering wheel curls
around your chest, you and Mel
are singing in the back of an ambulance,
let me go home and start over.

4.

Twenty years later I hit you,
the train least expected.
I love how we collide. All night,
wine, the showing of scars.
This is where I fell when I was four,
this is where they cut
you open, spent six hours picking out
the splinters of your femur.

I kiss scars. I am
a train softly crossing
the wounds of a man who died
for two minutes and returned.

5.

Forty years later you will still
know the facts. Your truck laid
fifty-one feet of rubber, hit
the twenty-seventh car
of a fifty-four car freight train
and the twenty-eighth
knocked you into a field.

I am a train rolling
around you in this prairie bed.
When the cop and the brakey
pried you out I was dreaming
of this.

BARBARA KLAR WAS BORN in Saskatoon and attended the University of Saskatchewan. Her previous book, *The Night You Called Me A Shadow*, also published by Coteau, was co-winner of the Gerald Lampert Award for best first book of poetry in Canada in 1993. It also received the Saskatchewan Writers Guild manuscript award in 1991. Retired from treeplanting in four Canadian provinces, Barbara now lives in the village of Ruddell, Saskatchewan, with her partner Hal and their hound dog.

ACKNOWLEDGEMENTS

THE AUTHOR THANKS the Saskatchewan Arts Board for a grant to shape this book. Thanks also to the Saskatchewan Writers Guild, the Sage Hill Fall Poetry Colloquium, and the late Saskatchewan School of the Arts. Thanks to Gerry Hill for his field work, his insights, eyesights, and faith in risk. Thanks to Susan Andrews Grace, Sara Cassidy, Pam Galloway, Tim Lilburn, Ruth Roach Pierson, Steven Ross Smith, and Paul Wilson for various encouragements. Thanks to Hal for his love, patience, and support, and especially seeing past the darknesses.

Incarnations of some of these poems have appeared in *Grain, Museletters,* and *NeWest Review.*

The title and italicized terms in *The Classification Of Snow* are from Edward. R. LaChapelle's *A Field Guide to Snow Crystals,* (Vancouver, J.J.Douglas, 1969).

Two lines in *Nine Reasons* are borrowed from Hal Gates.